Making Honey

Did you know honey bees make honey?

The *honey* **bees** go flower to flower, finding "**NECTAR.**"

The **NECTAR** is in the bottom of the flower in the *nectar sack.*

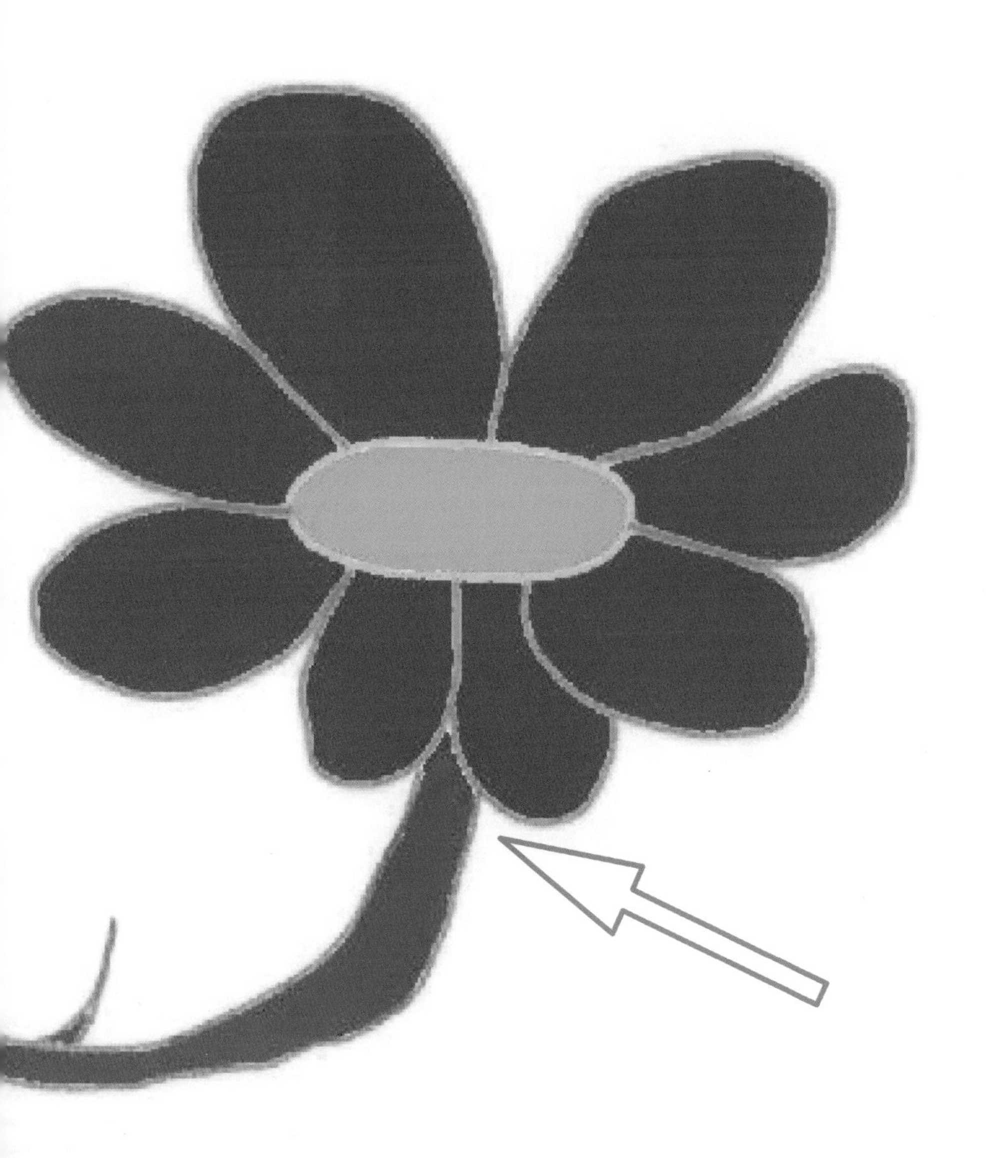

The honey bee's tongue is very **long** and folds out.

The Honey Bee sticks her long tongue into the flower to suck the liquid nectar sugars.

The bee’s long tongue is connected to 2 stomachs, the regular stomach and the **HONEY STOMACH**.

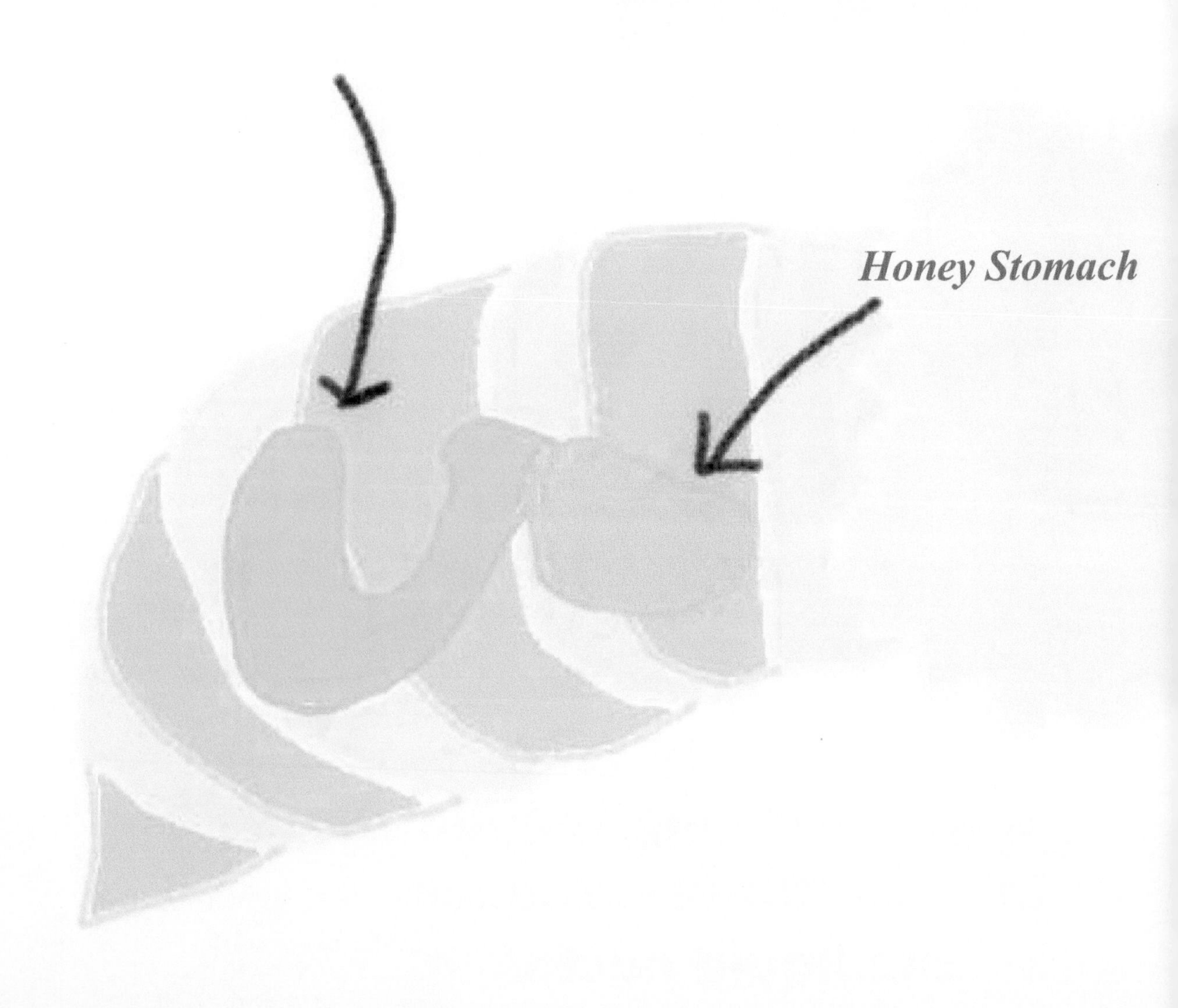

The Honey Stomach has enzymes that literally change "nectar sugars" into "honey sugars."

First,

The enzymes in the honey stomach make the nectar sugars fall apart and become smaller pieces. Water starts falling out of the nectar sugars as the pieces fall apart, so the nectar sugars becomes thicker.

All of this is happening in the honey stomach while the bee goes flower to flower to collect enough nectar to fill up her honey stomach.

When she is full, the honey bee goes back to the hive and she is greeted by her family of honey bees.

The honey bee's body is made to make honey so they must all work together to make enough honey to feed the hive.

The bees pass the thickened "nectar sugars" back and forth to each other through their long tongues.

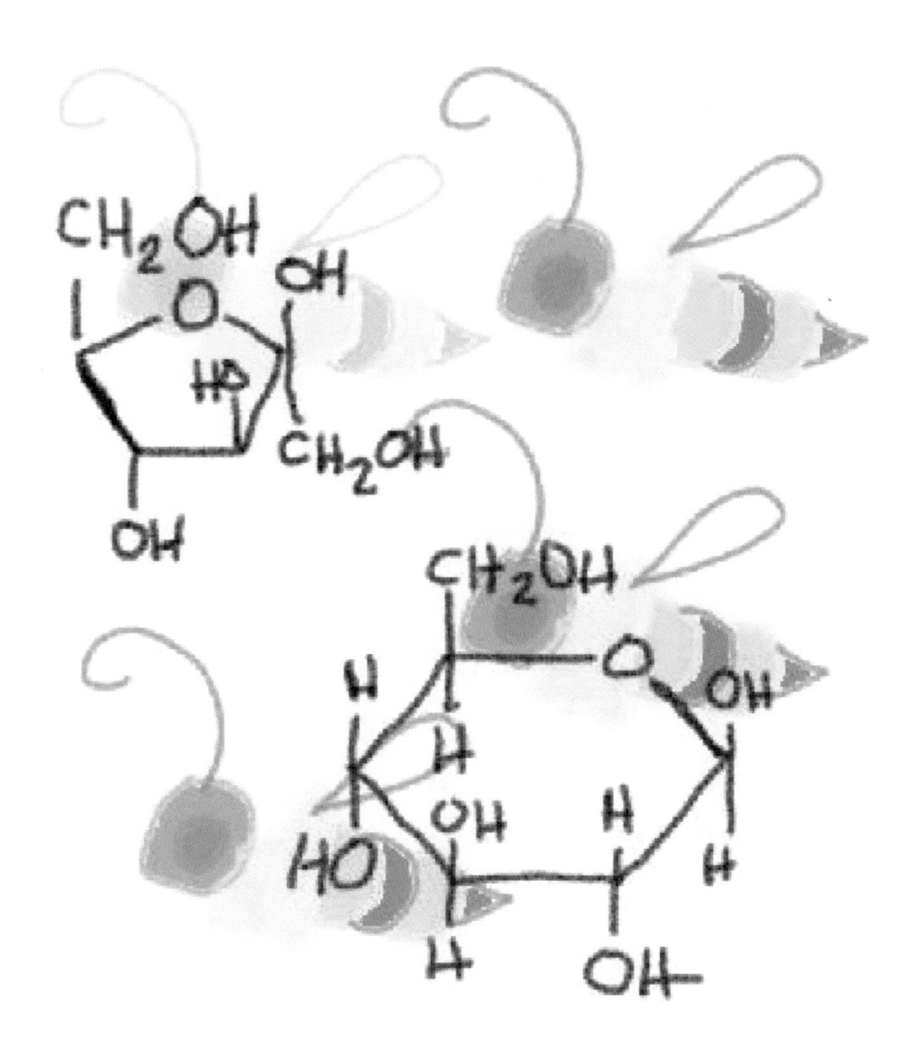

Each bee’s special honey stomach enzymes work together to continue to alter the “nectar sugar” and turn it into “honey sugar”.

The bees must do this until the molecular formula of the "nectar sugar" is changed into the molecular formula for "honey sugar."

Once the sugars are perfect, the bees place the liquid into the honey comb cells for safe keeping.

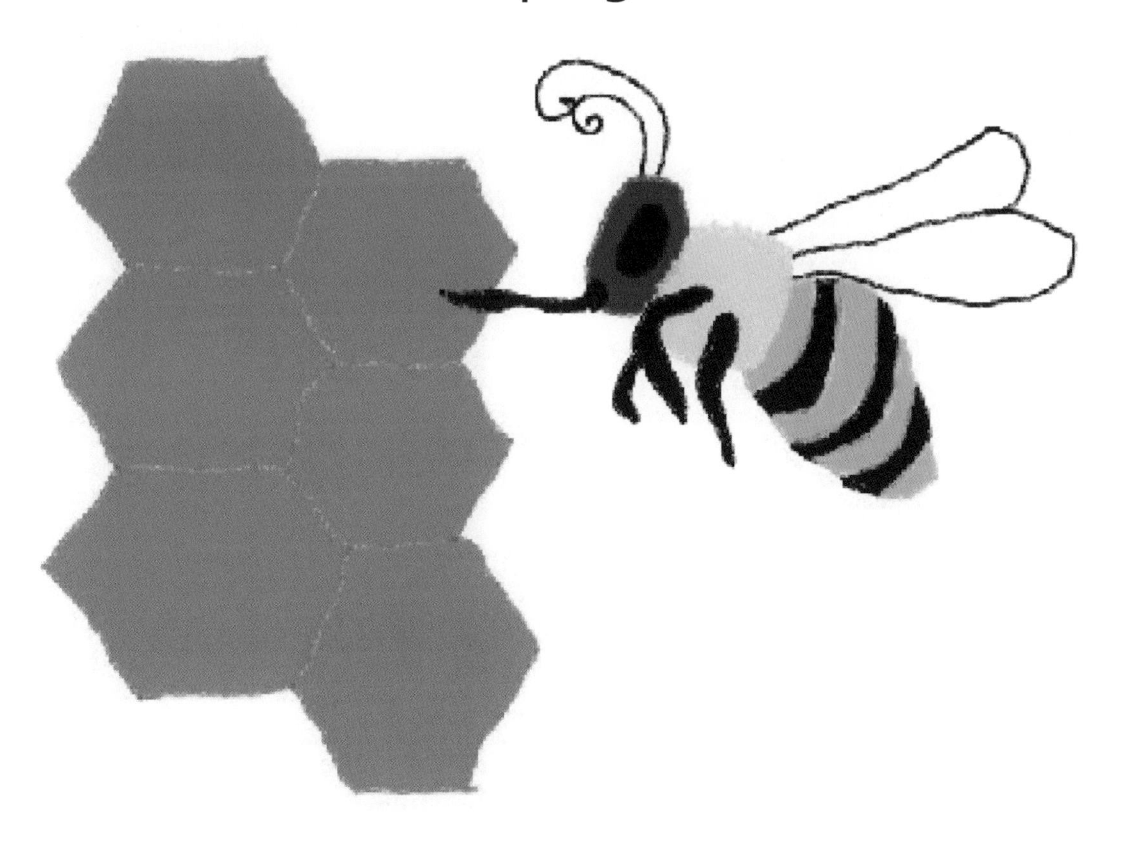

The nectar sugar is not honey yet!

At this stage, there is too much water! Honey is sticky so the bees must make the nectar liquid sticky like honey.

To make the nectar sugar mixture thick and sticky like honey, the bees remove water from the mixture by beating their wings very fast. The fast motion from the wings cause the hive to heat up. When the hive heats up, so does the honey.

When it's nice and hot, water begins to evaporate out of the "nectar sugar" molecules, changing the entire molecular formula of the liquid.

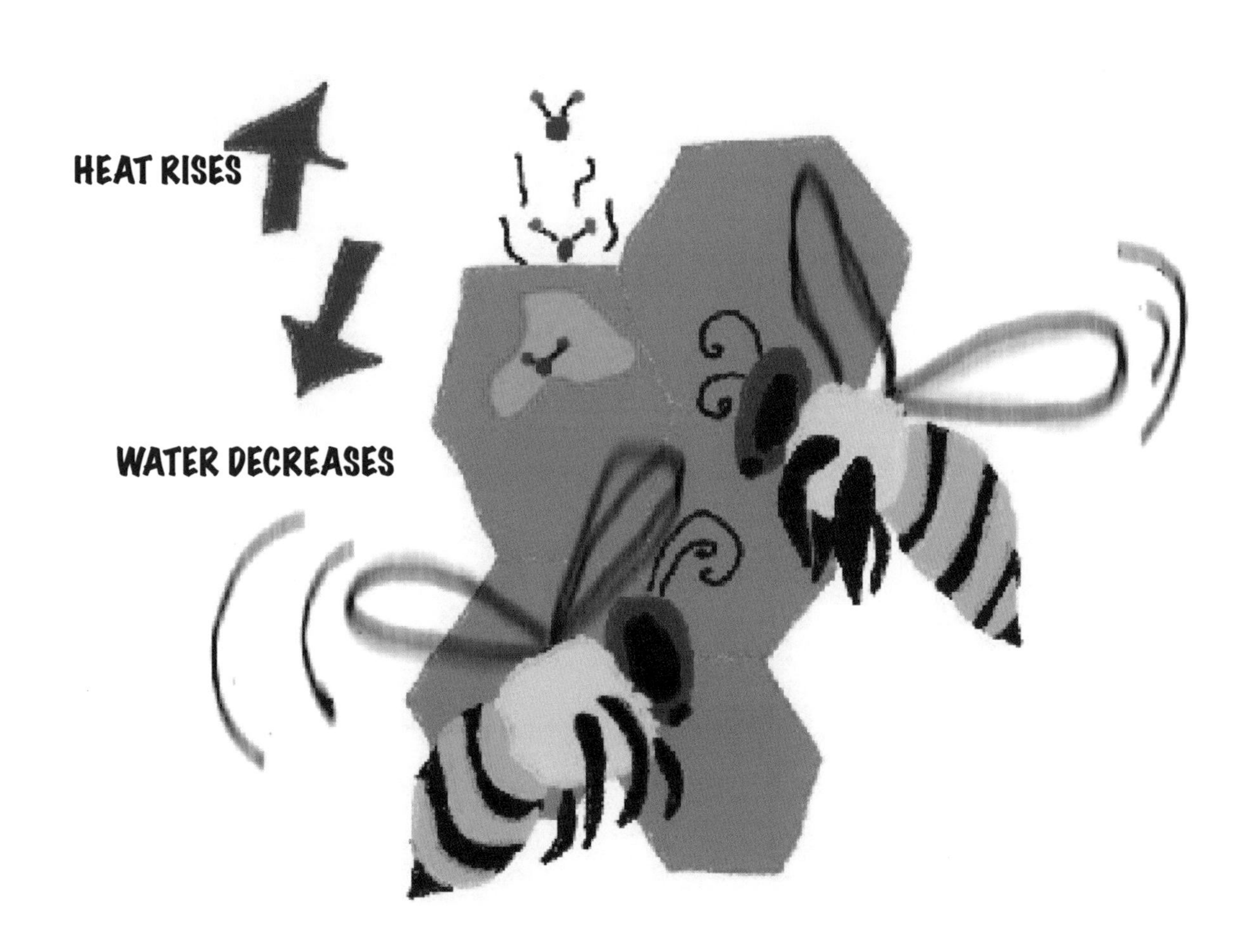

Evaporation is caused when heat is added to water.

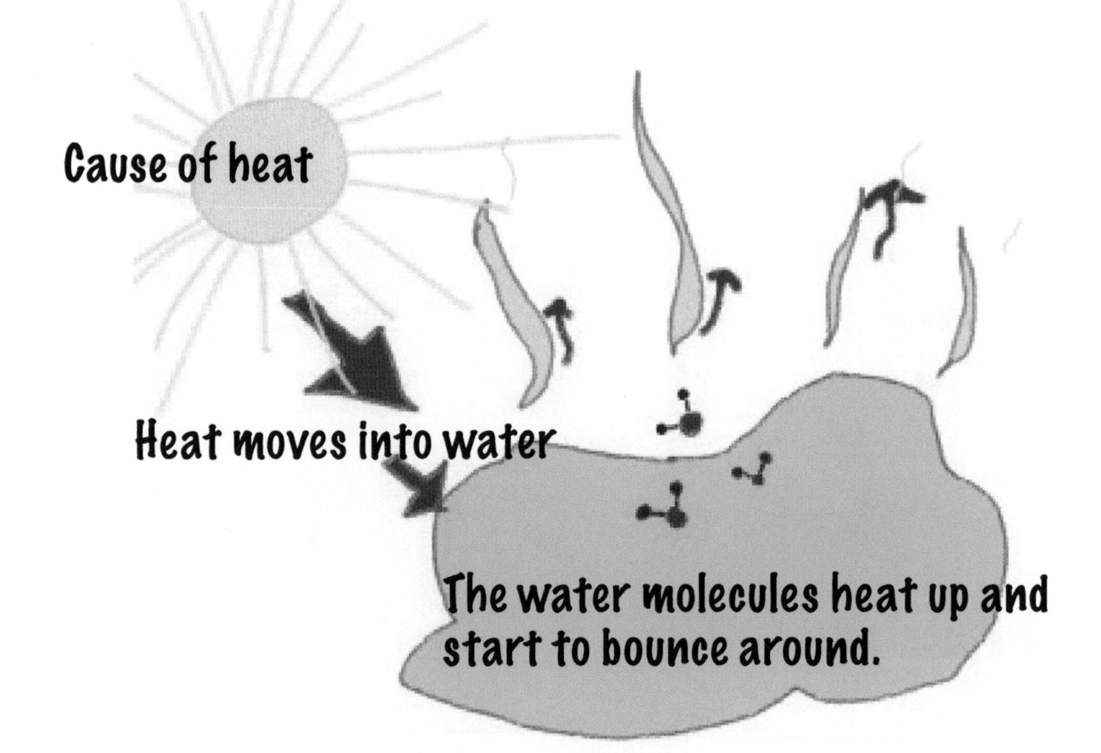

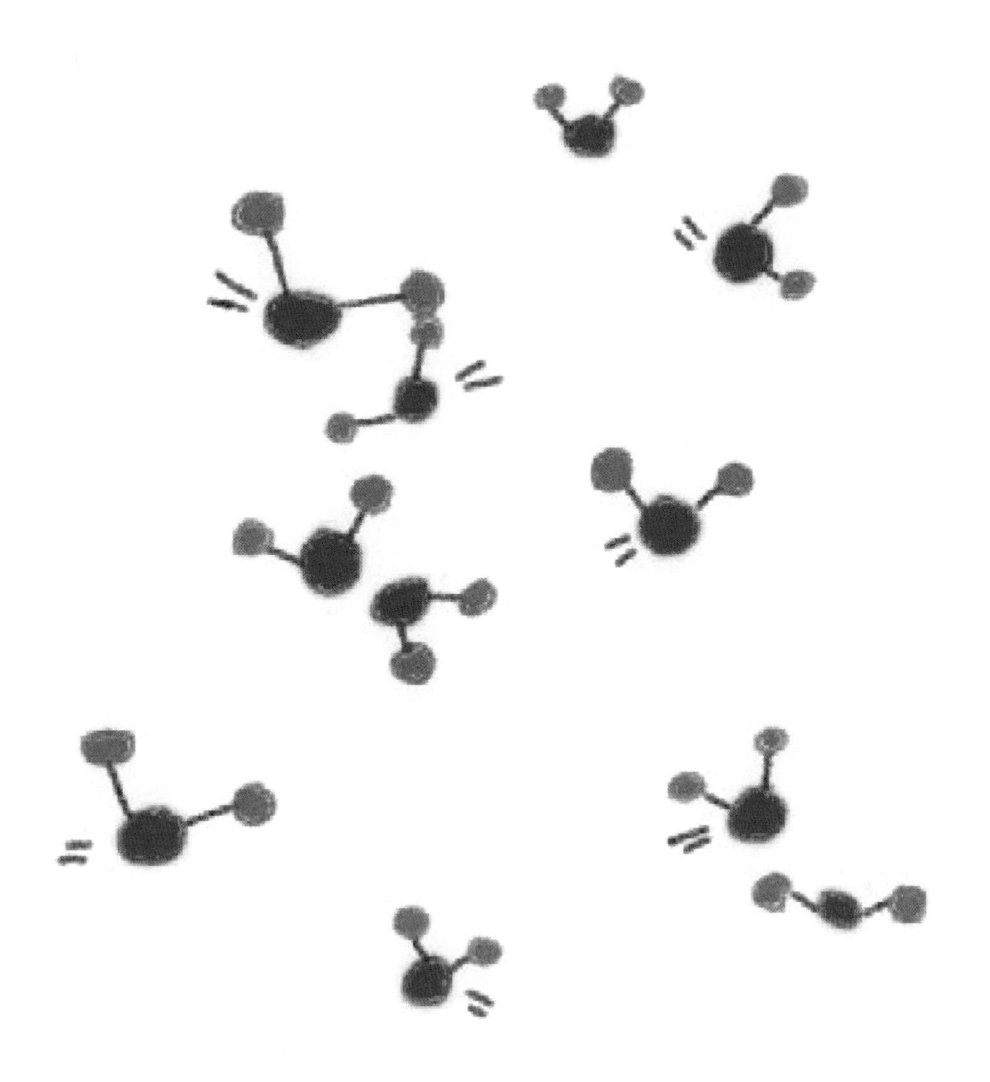

When water "evaporates,"
the molecules heat up and begin to bounce around until they change into gas. The gas then floats into the sky.

When full, the bees cap the honey comb cell with beeswax to protect the honey.

And Remember……
Honey never expires!!!

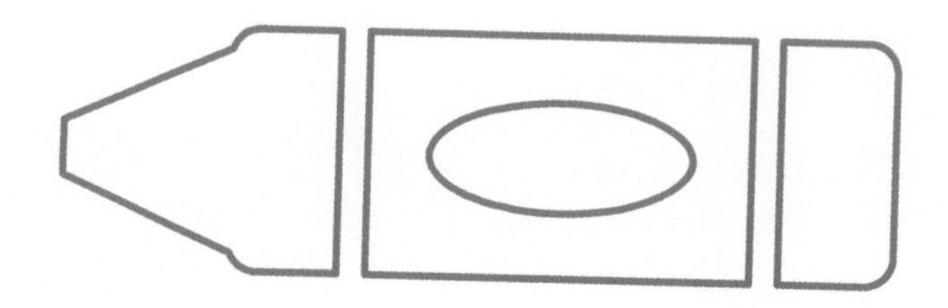

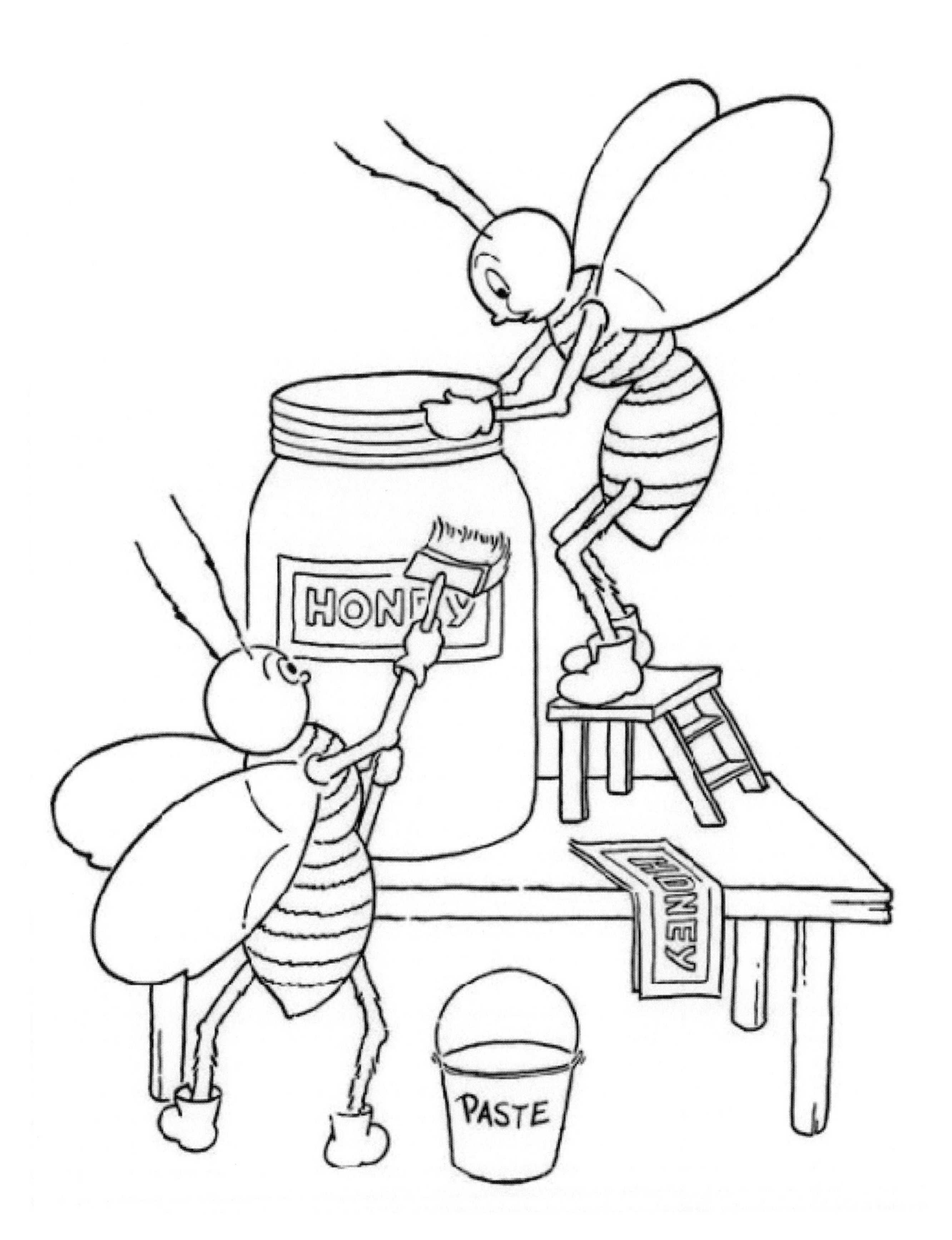
HONEY
PASTE

bee

Credit for coloring pages:

Lena London. *Honey bee photo by Charlesjsharp http://www.supercoloring.com/coloring-pages/honey-bee*

The Graphic Fairy. *https://pin.it/4ABPObg*

https://www.buzzaboutbees.net/bee-coloring-pages.html

Printed in Great Britain
by Amazon